WINTER OF WORSHIP

Also by Kayleb Rae Candrilli

Water I Won't Touch
All the Gay Saints
What Runs Over

WINTER OF WORSHIP

KAYLEB RAE CANDRILLI

Copper Canyon Press
Port Townsend, Washington

Cover art: Murmure Street, *Garb-age – Saynète 3 Slack*, 2021. Acrylic on canvas, 31.49 × 23.62 in.

Copper Canyon Press is in residence at Fort Worden State Park in Port Townsend, Washington, under the auspices of Centrum. Centrum is a gathering place for artists and creative thinkers from around the world, students of all ages and backgrounds, and audiences seeking extraordinary cultural enrichment.

LIBRARY OF CONGRESS CATALOGING-IN-PUBLICATION DATA
Names: Candrilli, Kayleb Rae, author.
Title: Winter of worship / Kayleb Rae Candrilli.
Description: Port Townsend, Washington : Copper Canyon Press, 2025. |
   Summary: "A collection of poems by Kayleb Rae Candrilli"—Provided by
   publisher.
Identifiers: LCCN 2024021853 (print) | LCCN 2024021854 (ebook) |
   ISBN 9781556596933 (paperback) | ISBN 9781619323018 (epub)
Subjects: LCGFT: Poetry.
Classification: LCC PS3603.A5374 W56 2025 (print) |
   LCC PS3603.A5374 (ebook) | DDC 811/.6—dc23/eng/20240513
LC record available at https://lccn.loc.gov/2024021853
LC ebook record available at https://lccn.loc.gov/2024021854

9 8 7 6 5 4 3 2 FIRST PRINTING

COPPER CANYON PRESS
Post Office Box 271
Port Townsend, Washington 98368
www.coppercanyonpress.org

for friends here, and in the hereafter

Don't listen to me; my heart's been broken.
I don't see anything objectively.

Louise Glück

CONTENTS

WINTER OF
WORSHIP

FROM ABOVE

It's a new year, and each oyster I open re-injures
my two-seam shoulder, my curveball bones.

At the baseball fields, we believed in both
pearls and the American dream. At the baseball

fields, we were always almost abducted.
There, I ate only Swedish Fish, and kissed

the most beautiful girls, ducked behind dugouts.
I remember their flowering Nokia phone cases,

mainly, and how they all knew I was a boy
and whispered so. While I'm in the air, flying coach,

I still count the diamonds, each a gemstone
cut from the grassland. Each time I am

kissed, I smell sunflower seeds. I smell
yellow before she even arrives.

ONE HUNDRED DEMONS

My partner tells me I smell of vacation,

so: salt, cantaloupe, perhaps pine needles,

depending on the day. But back when

I was just a child in the woods, I woke every

morning to bad-hair days and mountain breath.

Rainwater collected in gullies of blue tarps

slung over cords of firewood, upturned lids

of trash cans, abandoned cement buckets.

I watched stagnant, ever-breeding mosquitoes

born to the hot greens of Pennsylvania

in summer. Each bite as insatiable and swelling

as the last. Before my parents burned

the hide of a poached bear, my jalapeño

garden burned bright with capsaicin.

Marco, our neighbor, showed me how

to tend the heat, and sat me down

to watch *The Godfather,* parts I through

III, *Casablanca* too. There are lessons

to be learned from the Italian men that find

family wherever they look. Twenty years

later, Marco will die from an unidentified

infection contracted on a Carnival Cruise

he waited decades to take. Alanis Morissette

ruined the meaning of irony, but isn't it ironic?

When my jalapeño garden died, all that remained

was rusty chicken wire snagging at my ankles—

sharp and nostalgic. When I left the mountain,

running from my father, I left behind:

books of fairies and dragons, bowls lined

with salvia resin. I slept in Sunnyside

Cemetery, and most nights my friend rolled

through the mausoleums in her convertible,

blasting Kid Cudi's *Man on the Moon.* You

have often been exactly where you belonged.

If you believe nothing, believe that.

My hometown has always worn its own

breed of hackles, as many hometowns do,

bristling at strangers. Roman drifted,

coming through, just to leave. We worked

as mascots for a tax agency, the 2009 season.

Imagine us there, an offshoot of Route 6

in rural America, a queer and a drifter dressed

as statues of liberty—dancing. Ten dollars

an hour will always be ten dollars

an hour. Behind the Little League fields,

we smoked salvia, split headphones strung

from my iPod classic. After tax season,

as Roman left town, I tucked the iPod

in his jacket pocket. I think of him still,

on a Megabus, listening to Daft Punk.

Had I ever been less myself, I might have

run my fingers through his curled hair.

I love the men that never ventured

to love me the most. I love the men who

saw me as myself before I did. Called me

dude, and *man,* and just passed the bowl.

Before all the drugs were laced, the acid

was pure as a lake frozen over. Before

fentanyl poured through the ports,

the ecstasy rolls were only ever a little dirty.

It's best to never tempt fate. It's best

to always take note of the stars' positions

in the sky. Once, in the early 2000s, my family

visited our long-abandoned storage unit.

Inside, a Furby born of the '90s

was still chirping. To speak of curses

is so often hyperbole. To speak of witchcraft,

so often taboo. The 1990s prayed only

to god, the Pink Panther, and the Energizer

Bunny. Unnerving is Furby, speaking only

to itself for a decade. Unnerving is my baseball

cards sticky with the raw sour of mouse

urine. Who knows what becomes of hurt

when it no longer hurts. In the clearing

behind my childhood home, a marble

headstone and my mother's guard

of gargoyles—their eyes gray in December,

gray in June. No matter. Each Fourth of July

my mother would bring kitchen shears

on a ride through the backroads, trimming

tiger lilies from road shoulders. She'd fill

her marble urns, tuck the sunburnt lilies

behind the ears of her gargoyles. Please

know, most trans boys have spent their lives

swimming through the story of Peter Pan.

Tiger Lily, Captain Hook, and Peter—

Peter, young and boyish for all of time.

Once, my sibling wrote to the local country

music radio station, and won a limousine

ride to dinner, then to Cathy Rigby's farewell

tour as Peter. My father's OxyContin

put him to sleep in his penne. The whites

of his eyes reflected the lost boys, swinging

through the rafters of the Scranton

Cultural Center. A woman playing a boy,

Shakespearean. Shakespearean, a father

unaware of the damage only a father can do.

What's done is done, unless you give it a pulse

to breathe with. Each morning, I think about

the ice caps, sweating. The seagulls are moving

inland, and they feel the heat humans refuse

to feel. This is almost all I know to be true.

The seagulls are getting mouthy

and I don't blame them. Tectonic

plates, tectonic popcorn in the sandy mouth

of a gull. On vacation, my partner and I held

engagement rings in our pockets, pizza

in our hands. When the gulls came

down, we couldn't even see the sun.

GHAZAL WRITTEN FOR THE LIDS IN DOWNTOWN BROOKLYN WHERE I CHOSE MY NAME

I grew up poor, no monogrammed bath towels or duffle bags, nowhere to travel but into myself.
My mountain had so many small mountains inside it, and I had breasts. If I had to give myself

any name then, it would have been *hunter* or *whittler* or *fire with only flint*. Of course, I was stronger
than I should have been. Strength is the nature of a trans boy huddled over kindling, lighting themselves

up into only ever embers. Sometimes I still feel like a woman, and, really, it's not so bad if I'm alone.
I don't want to live forever, but I want to live long enough to make people upset. It's so easy to lose myself,

whispering sweet incantations for all gorgeous trans boys left dying in forests. O winter of worship,
I've pretended plenty, and lying to my mother, if only for a few decades, was intended as a deeply selfless

thing. I don't remember knowing my name until I knew it—a partner told me to keep the *y* and that was it—
Kayleb, monogrammed onto a leopard-print flat brim. Yes, it's okay to love what you love. If I had to ask myself

anything, I'd ask, Did this poem touch all it was asked to touch? Did it hold out its hand and offer something? Did it ask, How long does this new name have?
I'd ask, How about the length of my lifeline?

A POEM ABOUT ONLY BASEBALL

Bubba, together out there
on the diamond,

you were always shining
brightest. I remember

you catching a pop fly,
then rolling your body

right into a front flip.
God, we were just

children and the world
was ours and we couldn't

be hurt even when we were
hurt or hurting. Every small

town has a story about a
talented and beautiful boy

who smolders. I was
the only girl on the Little

League team, and though
I am no longer a girl,

you were always so fiercely
soft with me. When I lost

my teeth at second base,
you searched the rocky

infield dirt and told me
not to worry about the money

it would cost to put me
back together. I think

about your daughters often,
and I want to pass down some

of the gentleness you gave me.
I keep it all in my wallet, still,

tucked between receipts and
the coordinates of our town—

our town that takes all the good
ones, and never looks back.

DAYTONA 500

Where we're from, we know ballet as Dale Earnhardt
gliding through the traffic of Daytona; we know dance

as our hands moving across a table of drunk Miller Lites.
This is universal because I say it is. When my mother called

me Kayleb for the first time, I remembered the haunted house
on Clifton Hill, how she was tugged away by a hired actor.

I screamed until they took us out the fire escape. To care
is to call a name. To care is to call your mother's name, as

your father pulls at her ankles. Dear Ma, you know your
hands were always too blue in the winter, strapping snow

chains onto the Ford Expedition. This is a happy memory
because it's a memory. It is warmer now. Blame global

warming, blame the divorce. It doesn't matter. All that
matters is the heat of the sun, and both being here to feel it.

ARS POETICA

When Whitney died,
I played her greatest

hits through the late shift
at the hookah bar—tobacco

smelling of mint, rose, and sex
on the beach. When friends

die, I don't cry until the longhand
elegy—such wet ink, a river

of grief that runs south to north.
There is a strawberry Starburst

wrapper floating in a puddle.
There is a reason for each life

raft tossed into turbulent water.
There is a reason we've all

been so imprecisely scrawled
into the mirror's steam.

A POEM ABOUT BATMAN

Davy, my whole family is looking
for dimes so they can feel you.

They have a few dollars saved, and
even I keep a few, Roosevelt side up

on the mantel. It's a small thing, all
those dimes. They don't pay the bills

piling up on your father's kitchen counter,
but they mean something—something

about the afterlife, something about
how family always searches, even when

everyone knows, maybe, the search
should be given up. But nobody quits

on you, Davy, not when you were alive,
or this February, as another year

without you rolls around. Me and you
never really got along, but nothing

matters less when it comes to family.
We once watched the Chicago Bears

tight end break his leg so gruesomely
that we reached for each other, hand

in hand on the basement futon. I will
remember you just like this, empathetic,

and feeling pain that isn't yours to feel.

FOR MAC MILLER AND 2009

Imagine, you're on a bicycle and the wind
is behind you, and you're pedaling fast

on bald tires through an imagined blue world.
Between the stratus clouds there is no such thing

as fentanyl—no light dusting in your coke,
or in the next cloud on your left, which may,

one day, become a Pittsburgh snowstorm.
Humans have created all types

of afterlives, and this bike ride on a bed
of clouds is what I imagine for all my dead.

I often wish I had met my partner even
sooner; I wish I could go back and find

my way into one of their late-night drives,
swimming around the New Jersey suburbs—

find my way into the backseat, listen
to "Senior Skip Day," and admire the pattern

of each fingerprint. We all want to cheat
something, and I'd cheat time for just

a single extra moment, to feel the bends
of one extra backroad together. I wish

I could have met all my partner's friends
before they died. We are too young

to know so much about life without
our friends. We look to the stratus

clouds and every day
we learn more.

A MARBLE RUN FOR THE LIGHTS

for Steph

I.

Such a cliché to write a poem for a dead friend. I don't know much about stage lights or undiagnosed heart problems besides how they burn,

too bright. I don't know much, but I know I wish I could have shined a light into your chest & seen it coming. What we don't know can't hurt

us, until we are hurting. I know that in a world where you are not dead, we can take Yesterday to the forest & hold her hostage for just one

more summer. In a world where you are not dead, we head to the woods & skin the wildflowers of their thin, delicate fur. I wish

human skin were thicker & less delicate. Sometimes, I leave the faucet running & everything is figurative until the ceiling is caving.

Everything is figurative until you are falling through the waterlogged floor & your friends are gone. I know as much about hurt as anyone,

but no more. I drink hurt like the ground takes in its rain. We all do. I once watched you rebuild your '67 Dodge Dart on a South Philly

side street. I watched you hold the engine in your hands like a heart, as the Philly litter swirled around us—confetti or piñata or small cyclone.

The wind in this city grows a garden of tiny trash twisters, up like tulips every May. It really is beautiful. None of us are getting any younger.

II.

I'm not getting any younger & it is probably time to get my alcoholism in check. I can always taste champagne & my partner's worries.

My partner worries about my body & each unpredictable tide inside it. I drink through the blush-warm seawater &

I drink too much warm beer. I don't blame anyone for their drinking. It's easy to guess where it comes from. Familiar nectar, familiar fruit.

Familial neglect. Familial fruits. I once took a broken lightbulb from its socket with a kiwi & replaced a bulb that had burnt out years ago.

I replace each burnt bulb in our home & when my partner's heart murmurs, I feed them a plate of kiwi fruit, some sliced, tender potassium.

Tender & simple, my grandfather loved JuJuBes & vodka cranberries. When he died, he first died surrounded by merpeople in his pool.

When he died second, he died surrounded by his children. Though time isn't linear, we hope it will be. Every ocean love story is essential

to our survival—& though time isn't linear, I hope the merpeople are braiding my grandfather's hair & I hope the starfish is set to marry

the sand dollar. I want my hair braided again. I want to marry my partner. I want all of my dead to come to the wedding & throw milkweed.

III.

My friend, I wish you could see the wedding, toss milkweed into the air for the monarchs & just party. You told me first that happiness

was a worthwhile endeavor. You were the first to point to my partner & say, Why not just be happy? You once hit a speed bump at 70 mph

& that's when I knew I wanted to live. You once poured a beer over the balcony for my first friend gone. When you died, we searched

for the photos. When you died, we dug through the years & found you only behind the shutter. The moon is always recalling the friends

I dream of. The moon chants your name & tries to teach me about lights & electricity & faulty engines because you're not here to do it.

Because you're not here to do it, we have to learn to be good people all by ourselves. We have to stare into the lights & hit our marks.

When I stare into the sun, I can feel the wildflowers growing taller. The monarchs are struggling to get to Mexico, but still they manage.

We are struggling to get where we are going, but still we try, if only for you. I will collect all the grasses' dew in jam jars & pour it out.

If only for you, I will pour a beer off my balcony. It's such a cliché to write a poem at all, but, my friend, I do hope you can hear it.

SILENT LIGHT

In the early 2000s, Pennsylvania's only light at night came

from Walmart flashlights and the gentle throb of heat lightning—

casting shadows over hay bales. On weekends, spotlights shone

out the backs of Chevrolets—deer and owls kept their eyes open.

Beer cans crushed into coins, rural currency. It was a simple time,

though everyone I knew was being abused. Twenty years later,

my partner, who loves only me and the New Jersey tides, sees heat

lightning—for the first time, from our city veranda—breaking like glass

between buildings. My partner pours out a glass of wonder. The air

is hot and delightful. Recipe is as recipe does. All the world's

landscapes make all the world's humans. You should know the truth.

When it all ends, all we'll have is the high tide, and the heat, and

such wonder for how we loved. Such wonder at what we've done.

ANOTHER POEM ABOUT CORNFIELDS

for Shana & Pulse

We worked the hookah bar together for years,
tossed rose shisha into clay bowls and lit it up.

We sold bongs to kids on their 18th birthdays,
but called them *water pipes,* with authority

and know-how. After work, at three a.m., we'd
pile into your car, and you'd just drive. We'd cut

through the Pennsylvania cornfields and we'd
trace the long and winding tube of the Milky Way

with our too-stoned fingers pointing through
your wide-open sunroof. When I was young

I drank three bottles of Delsym cough syrup
a day. And so did you. This is just one

of our dark and orange-flavored addictions.
We shared Coricidin, Benadryl, and booze

too. We never spoke about the hurt behind
it all, because why bother. Some truths aren't

even worth the breath. When you died, so did 49
other beautiful people in an Orlando nightclub.

You would have hated to know they were gone.
You would have hated living a single moment

in the world without all those young and vital
queer people. I miss you; I miss them. There's

a photo I keep, and it's you on Halloween
in a green and purple bejeweled mask, looking

more like yourself than I'd ever seen you.
What else is there to say? I remember

the stars, and the corn, and all of you.

I WISH I WERE MORE LIKE MY MOTHER

and asked, *Pardon me?* rather

than shouting, *What?* but it's hard

to break old habits and move

through the world using only

gentle consonants. Every night,

my mother read me *Dr. Seuss's*

Sleep Book and spread baby

powder around my bed to ward

off the wolf spiders, but they wolfed

around anyway, our house nestled

in the Pennsylvania woods. I would

prefer to be a person with rational

fears. I would prefer to have remained

my mother's daughter, too. But no

animal lingers while a brush fire

rages. Everyone tries to stay alive,

vital and clawing just a little longer.

ALL IN RED

The sun is drifting away again, behind clouds
that look most like the hairs well sprung

from my temples. I can't see the sun setting,
but I know it is. So many things are like this:

merely a sensation of truth. I can't see my body
changing, but I know it already is. Just as I know

there's a woman at the benches on Bainbridge
Street, though I am not there with her.

She is thumbing through a stack of photos
of her son, printed on copy paper,

kept quarter-folded in her purse. I know
that her son is adored, though I sense

he does not. I know that my masculinity
is a fragile and delicate thing. I refuse all

glasses with stems. I've always been clumsy
with a sense of strength that I may or may

not have. My partner says: *Your handwriting*
looks like you grew up in the forest, like worm-

wood, or bark and brambles. I fell a tree
in a suburban New Jersey township

and my partner tells me I've never looked quieter,
or less furrowed, even as my hands bleed

from some gnashing saw teeth. In another
suburb, one hundred miles northwest,

my mother keeps my comic book collection,
safe and organized in her closet, even though

I am 31 with a house of my own. When
I visit, I flip through the covers: *Machine Man*

2020, the Jetsons in their flying hatchbacks.
We are living in the future now and over

the weekend I teach AI about trans bodies,
and it learns so much faster than family,

or the men at my favorite dive bars. I ask
AI to show me a trans man in a red river

of lily pads, and it is impossible not to feel
seen, and in Technicolor at last. When I tell

my grandmother that I've gone to collect
the vial and syringes that will raise my blood

pressure, damage my liver, stubble my face,
she tells me she visited my great-grandmother,

who has begun to blink with a distinct and deadly
forgetfulness. She tells me my great-grandmother

either knew me as my gender or didn't know me
at all. Perhaps if the whole world knew me

either correctly or not at all, it would feel softer.
Down the street, a neighbor I never met passed

in the early morning. He was just 40, and looking
out from my window, I see his son, just 9,

walking home from school. On New Year's Eve,
confetti rains down around his home, his family.

My dog watches the fireworks from the window
with wonder, all of his fear absolved by the exploding

colors he may or may not see. What a strange
world of sensations this is: falling asleep

to a movie you did not pick, the burn of a button
on your forearm straight out of the dryer,

the rustle of scratched lottery tickets mixed
with a few brittle fall leaves. In South Philadelphia,

my neighbors use tape to tie their garbage bags:
duct, masking, packing. These are regionalisms,

just the same as crayfish or crawfish. Crick
or creek. They look so beautiful and practiced

as they toss the ponytailed bags off their stoops,
their free hand waving in a grandchild from

the street as the sun we cannot see, sets.
I am so unpracticed at being neighborly. But still

I worry after Vicky's blood pressure without knowing
quite how to show it. I worry about my body changing,

and her, and Nancy, and Roe, knowing that I haven't
been a lady while shoveling three houses' worth of snow.

But winters have been mild, more mild each year,
even if the solstice darkness stays much the same.

In the dark, I've taken to oil painting, in mainly muddy
reds, rivers of crimson. The cops have taken to killing

climate activists. And I have taken to hiding
from my friends for years at a time. David Lynch

talks of living in fear during his time in Philadelphia,
and both my partner and I find this funny, not

necessarily because it's untrue but because where
haven't we lived in true and unadulterated fear?

My partner cries when they realize, soon enough,
they won't be able to protect me in the restroom.

And I would cry too if they weren't already wet
in my arms. Nothing I feel feels new, instead,

a raw and constant chafe, an always burning
yearn for the dead. But when my partner

and I fuck in the middle of the night, it is so circadian,
so early-human of us. There are no whispers of sonder.

No knowledge sans instinct. Really no fear, except
for all the carnivores braying outside our front door.

ELEGY FOR THE NOT YET DEAD RAINFOREST CAFE

It's a wild place, yes, but birthday parties are still thrown
and candles are still blown out, and thin streams of smoke
drift up into the cloudy, thundering ceiling. All most kids

ever want is a middle-class dinner out, with crayons
and spider monkeys swinging from the rafters. In Atlantic
City, as my partner and I order Cheetah Ritas and eat stale

nachos—on our one weekend vacation a year—I wonder
who will bankrupt first, the Olive Garden down the road
from my mother's little pink house, or every rainforest

in the world. There is only so much oxygen to go around,
and I wish I could explain to my dog why he doesn't have
a yard, and why he's on a leash, and why I cry in the winter,

when it isn't cold at all and it should be. There is so much
that needs explaining; like how, in some forests, the trees

grow so as to never touch one another—the canopy's
crown spinning a very shy web, but a web nonetheless.

A MARBLE RUN FOR THIS FINITE EARTH

I.

It is unbelievable to think my body could make another body under the right circumstances.

& under the right circumstances my body could build a skyscraper, but really, who has the time.

Who has the time nowadays to skyscrape, when even our bodies are too heavy for the earth. Each step

we take, the dirt beneath us bows to our weight. Close your eyes & you'll feel each coast sinking & if

you shut your eyes, you'll know not much matters anymore, only the way you kiss your partner's head. Who am I kidding,

so much still matters. You kiss your partner, you understand global warming & you've moved a bird with a broken wing

from the road. & when you moved that broken bird from the pavement, I bet you thought about your family & all

you are willing to do for them. I think about my family & still see the needle in my father's arm. Love is limitless.

Somewhere, still, there is a needle hanging from at least one of my father's veins. Please know, I would save him if I could.

II.

I would save every man from himself if I could. & please know, when I was young, I did terrible things on the internet.

The internet was young then & as terrible as it's ever been. Nobody is without reproach, or their own flavor of villainy.

Animals & children are beyond reproach, I suppose, but only barely & only until we teach them how to kill one another.

I once taught the neighbor boy how to kill a snake with the sharpened head of a shovel. If he remembers me at all,

he will remember me only for that one, cutting moment. I regularly dream I am killed by the bite of a black widow.

It is the dream I've dreamt since I was a child, almost weekly. It doesn't mean anything. But I am always afraid—

afraid of spiders, of dying any time before I am ready. Because of my father, I know more about pressure

points than one should. Because of my father, I know how to send a threat to sleep. I am not a violent person, so much as

I am a violent person when absolutely necessary. I am not above anything, other than the ground, for a little while longer.

III.

For a little while longer, I'll be here in a city, just above sea level. There is a trash bag stuck in the tree outside my window &

I'm irritated. But even the trash bag can be beautiful if I work hard enough. What is love besides letting me do some labor for you?

Let me do this labor for you, Love. I'll take out the trash. I'll make the bed. I'll build a model airplane & suspend it from the ceiling.

I'll string a plastic seagull from the banister & take you to the beach, at least twice each summer. I don't so much mind getting older

as I mind feeling older. At least once each summer, I dance in a field with my shirt off. I let the whole world stare at my scars. Why not?

Why not let the whole world stare at my body until it is unremarkable. Nearly all things smell the same when they rot: tulips, tongues.

I often bury tulip bulbs in the garden. Nearly everyone has spoken in tongues over a fresh grave. I wish my friends were still alive.

I really wish my friends were still alive. Every sunrise without them is a color I've never seen before. Not everyone is who they used to be.

Each sunrise I am thankful to see a day I've never seen before. Not everyone understands my body, but still, it's here & believable.

ON IMAGINING ARIANA GRANDE, BEFORE THE FAME, WORKING EVERY SUMMER AT RITA'S ITALIAN ICE

Not everyone is who they used to be;
even I wore too much eyeliner in 2007.

Even I was cruel to the first cute butch
girl that hit on me. I was scared of only

myself. I burnt myself with the Chi
hair straightener, and took Pink Pearl

erasers to my forearms and thighs.
So many of us did. Now, most of us

are who we always intended to be.
And some of us are dead. I regret

every unkind thing I've ever done, but
won't search for any forgiveness. Why

open a wound you hope has already
closed. After I came out, I got a job

as a side-street mascot. My old
friends threw pennies out their car

windows. And sure, they stung as they
hit, but I just listened to Lady Gaga

and imagined a different kind of body
for myself. I once told a girl I almost

loved that I could never love her.
I regret every time I slam a door,

not because the door is closed but
because of all that excessive noise.

HAIBUN FOR MY MOTHER AND THE EARLY 2000S

We draped our TV antenna with tinfoil, made the thing tendril out like Medusa and tuned in to *American Idol* every week. It's so vintage, to dial in to vote for a below-average singer, on the corded landline, again and again until we felt our voices heard. We all needed some democracy to get us through the week. Each week was harder than it should have been. But my mother has always seen the glass half full, even as she was beaten, even as her china was smashed on the floor, even as she was resuscitating my father again—his face ashy until it wasn't, his face dead until it wasn't. It's 2020 now, *American Idol* is still somewhere on the air, and the kids have brought tie-dye back. I folded each of my mother's seven tie-dye shirts every Sunday for years, felt the fabric thin between my thumb and forefinger. This is not a metaphor, though we were all fraying. There are no words to frame a mother's fatigue. My mother served dinner on paper plates, even though she knew the world was smoldering, even though she knew climate change would come for her children first.

Above the smoke I
smell only the ocean and
my mother's perfume.

GHAZALS CONNECTED AS THOUGH CARGO FREIGHTS

I.

Once, my mother boosted me into a dumpster of damp discarded library books. I fished out
limericks, and Langston Hughes, and stack after stack of *Hardy Boys*. Years later, when I came out

to my mother, behind a closed door, I cried like a wolf. I didn't know it then, but there are queers all over
every forest, tucked in hunting blinds, hands huddled around portable propane heaters. Their hideout:

camouflage and venison jerky traded around like love letters. But even Pennsylvania folk in love are taken
by windstorms. When I say wind, I mean debris, and when I say debris, I mean the Oxy scrips handed out

once every two weeks, by a doctor in each and every county. I remember those car rides with my father—
me and my sibling sweating in the back, asking for Burger King, or to turn up U2's "Beautiful Day," or to get out

and stretch in the Salvation Army parking lot. My father was named after his father, and his father named
after his. Peter, from Latin for "stone." Too stoned and swerving. Every headlight on this backroad is burnt out.

II.

When my mother was a young mother, she would sunbathe naked on the porch. Personal planes would fly over, lower and lower, dangerously close to the treetops. As she bronzed in baby oil, I searched for four-leaf clovers

and thought about all the girls I had already decided I loved. I would whittle them tokens of affection and hope they might finally see me. Just after I made my body angular enough to stop bleeding, I had my first sleepover.

We talked all night, and right before bed, we traced one another's lips with our pointer fingers. In the morning we were silent but took pictures of one another lying dangerously across train tracks. Tenderness boils over

if you're not careful. Tenderness is all over the stovetop. Tenderness is two girls in love but unable to say why. Once, I climbed a trestle and threw wildflowers into coal freights as they rattled by, one for each undercover

trans child in my hometown. You should know that I would save them all if I could. When I rolled up my sleeves and became a boy, I didn't lose an ounce of gentleness. So, what's your new name? It's not over until it's over.

III.

The Alabama Amtrak whistles each night, loud and bossy through the kudzu, on its way to New Orleans. Take the Crescent line and all you see is green and porch swings. When I made a home of the South, I was taken

under its arm, like any other cousin. I was invited into dart leagues and nobody much cared about my body, only that I could throw, even while drunk and bumpy with mosquito bites. I've made so many mistakes

in my life, but none when naming my friends. When I was a kid, after each rainstorm I'd search for fire newts— bright and humid animals. When I was a kid, I tinkered with the tinfoil antenna, and envied the Undertaker's

muscles. What boy didn't? So much about the world has changed since then, but I still learned the most useful thing you can do with your time is throw milkweed for the monarchs and keep your friends close. Please take

my word for at least that. Each morning, I pray to a floral god; I pray for my friends' houseplants and I pray for their growth. Friend, if you need me, I can kiss your cheek, and suggest a train you might like to take.

IV.

Even though the only blood I've ever had on my hands is my own, it's still hard to sleep. When my father
slept, he slept with his eyes open, the whites of them glowing in the almost moonlight. So many fathers

are worried that their families will escape in the night, cut their losses and just run. You might think I'm angry,
but I'm angry only when the engines won't start and we need them to. Someone should tell our forefathers

about all their indelible and violent mistakes. Someone should tell them about all the American children in danger
and bleeding. Tell them each botched prosecution is another hollow point thrown in a fire for later. So many fathers

know they've done wrong but won't admit a thing, and instead roll their trucks drunk into another cornfield. Instead
blame their wives, who were at home the whole time. Instead say, *Look at me when I'm talking to you. I'm your father.*

Somewhere, on a property that once belonged to my family, a light green house is rotting fast into the hillside.
The Candrilli Construction sign, crooked and rusty. Teens break in to tell ghost stories. They still name my father.

V.

My mountain had no wolves but plenty coyote, plenty of paper birch taken down by the wind. I used to name every fallen tree, each coyote mounted on the wall. Now, when I wake, I wake next to my partner. I roll their name

into the bedsheets—like a color poured into a glass of water. Our life is full of plenty and we built it this way. We plot our future on graph paper and fill it in with scented markers. We draw up a list of brand-new surnames

and try them on like you would a new pair of high-tops; everything chafes at first. But there's no need to worry. Around here, the waves aren't made of porcelain. So, don't worry about them breaking. I can't wait to name

all my partner's kindnesses as we deliver our vows: all the milkweed thrown, all the lights strung and floating, all the Jiffy Pop and tenderness. And perhaps, at the wedding, I'll mention that nobody needs their deadname

at all. My father was named after his father, and his father named after his. I named myself. Perhaps destiny is a myth, and perhaps this myth is all we have. It's time to call me by my name. Please don't miss a sound.

Y2K IN NEPA

This century only truly began
when my mother threw the milk,
the cream cheese, the butter.
I dodged each as they spread
like wine over the love seat,
ran like years dripped off the back
of the couch. The fourth wall,
we know, is built to be broken.
My father ripped Exit signs
from movie theaters. Whispered
fire. Cinema is as cinema does.
Beside my bed, pill bugs, and
opioids hidden from all the fathers
of the world. Each window
is at least three colors of violet,
of violence. I'm sure of nothing.
Who can say different?

THE ONLY ATLAS WE NEED IS ONE DRAFTED BY CHILDREN

I know, because a woman told me,

Even a horse's shoe against stone

can spark a fire that wilds too far.

All humans have forged in the embers

combusts, eventually. The copper busts

of men who believed only in genocide

are common as clouds. The barrels

of .357s were born red-hot, before

they tucked themselves into angry

men's waistbands. Yes, I write

about my body because nobody

wants me to have one. This is not

a lonely life. This is the truth of all

people I have kissed, under the shade

of weeping willows. In Pennsylvania,

we are known to gamble our money

as much as our lives: scratch-offs,

Powerball, lifting rocks to wrestle

both king and coral snakes. *Red*

touching black, safe for Jack. Red touching

yellow, kill a fellow. Children in a forest

depend on verse, limerick, the iambs

of wind throbbing through birch trees.

Across the country, my desert family

drinks exclusively Pacifico, and grafts

the wounds of cacti—two species eager

to grow as one. This is all to say, most

people understand more about transness

than they let on. My small town let me

play baseball with the boys, let me

dodge the goose shit littering right field,

and let me lead off. All transgression

of gender permissible, if I batted over

.300, listened to 3 Doors Down, Creed,

and supported the war. What comes first,

the hatred or the curriculum to teach it?

I memorized four centuries of papal

reign before the periodic table. I knew

atomic warfare before the atoms bumping

together to build it. I learned I was alive

before I learned how I became so—

parents all atomic and chafing. Some

things are inevitable, like rain in April,

a teenager's newfound lust, and disease

dancing through a child's poorly tended

ant farm. Somewhere, a child is playing

cartographer in the woods—making

maps of worm writing. Somewhere,

that child marks the roads we should

have taken, in only tempera paint.

RAIN IN APRIL

I am old enough now that friends have bloomed

into parents. I imagine the trouble they will have

with their mouthy teens and feel hopeful, for just

a moment. I am old enough that friends

have tried and tried to conceive but cannot.

This world is built on synchronicity, but not

symmetry, and certainly not fairness. I am old

enough now that my friend has lost a child

to the heavy swing of bad chance. Once, years

ago at a synthy and glowing concert, that same

friend only wanted me on his tall and sturdy

shoulders so that he might train for his future

child—to practice the rarity of a gentle and safe

father. What I know now that I did not know

before: loss is such a rugged meadow of violets.

So here, in this rough meadow of meantime, let me

on your shoulders and I'll lift you onto mine.

We can parent one another, here, in this painful

grassland. We can wait here together for a new

season of wildflowers, as we remember the last.

POEM FOR THE START OF A NEW DECADE

It's a new decade and a new pandemic is roaring

through the world as I head to work at the fish-

market, to slice the heads off porgies, and snappers,

and bass—just to drop their beautiful, scaly,

surprised faces into the trash can. I do this

for too-delicate customers, who don't want

to see any eyes in their meals. I have never

understood this, or fully understood the speed

of a virus—the sheer sprint of it, as it trucks

through New York, to Hoboken, to Camden,

to Philly. I am worried for my smoker's lungs,

of course, but mainly worried for my grandmothers,

and the next-door neighbors, and everyone else.

The fragility of the world has always astounded me.

Off my veranda, I hear violin practice all day,

and even some piano—when the neighbor slides

open their backdoor. We aren't singing to one

another yet, but hopefully there will be more time

for that. The kids in the courtyard play hide-and-seek,

rather than smear-the-queer, for which I am thankful.

My rural town always preferred to shoulder-check

the queer right out of you. If I concentrate, I can

still feel the very gay wind rushing from my solar

plexus. I can still feel the red-hot peat moss shoved

into my mouth. But I can also still feel the very first

kiss with the very first girl I ever loved—hidden

behind her aboveground pool. Not all memories

are painful. Some feel just the same as they did

a decade ago—important and revelatory and sweet.

We understand our lives through that which we are given.

When both my sibling and I started smoking

too soon, they laid the ember of their Grape

Swisher Sweet on the petals of a dame's rocket

wildflower, and found the ember turned the violet

into a violent, unnatural teal. Beautiful and chemical.

When we returned to the flowers the next day,

the petals had shriveled, curled into small, dead

things. I spent five years estranged from my paternal

grandmother because I cried too hard over a bleach

stain on my favorite Harry Potter shirt. Neither of us

can get those years back, though we really are trying—

each phone call feels like a little less sand slipped

through our fingers. My grandfather and I used to

go bottle hunting in the woods behind his home.

Pull the smooth green glass of an old 7UP out

from the soft dirt like a weed. Sometimes aspirin

bottles, sometimes the amber glass of morphine.

Sometimes heroin. We'd drop the bottles all over

my grandmother's coffee table, and pill bugs would

crawl out, scuttle between the Styrofoam cups

filled with grounds. Five years after the message

is sent, on November 15, 2015, I find it

in my filtered messages on Facebook. Rita

Knight, whom I have never known, wrote,

Your grandfather Kenny is very sick. Please

call your grandmother. We have all missed

so much that we should not have missed.

Sometimes, my partner and I look over books

without reading a word. Our eyes seeing it all

but hearing nothing. It's a new decade, and though

I was taught to write poems that ignore technology,

I am still shuffling my last twenty dollars around

on Venmo, to some friends who need it more.

And I am re-listening to YouTube mixes that got

me through my early twenties—all electronica and

glitch step. It really doesn't matter how, or even if,

you survive, only that you tried. I send mix CDs

to my friends every new season, even though

no one really has a disk drive anymore. I'm told

it's the thought that counts most. Everyone I know

pitched in to help me remove my breasts

with a scalpel. And as the hospitals cancel all

surgeries to make room for what is coming,

I can't help but think about all the beautiful trans

people left to float in their bodies a little while

longer. Though the grocery store I work for

is mostly out of food, they still have some tulips—

so, I take those home in lieu of ground beef

and cucumbers. They sustain us, not the same,

but they brighten the place just enough. In Venice,

the water has cleared, and folks can see straight

to the bottom of the canal. I don't know a lot

about the world, but I could have predicted as much.

Take humans out of the water and watch it run clear.

My best friend is both a nurse and HIV-positive.

They've never seen themself the hero type, but

I imagine autumn will bring them new language

along with yellowing leaves. Have you noticed

yet that clouds move so much faster when you

watch them from your window? I want

to quit smoking, not so much for my health but

because it's the only thing I've ever done to hurt

my partner. It's a new decade, and most of my friends

are laid off, and the unusually clear water is rising

on all of us. What would you like me to say? I can't

internalize it all. Instead, I'll find some use for our

lemon rinds, I'll leave every violet flower untouched.

I'll think so much about the small and perfect shape

of my partner's engagement ring—upstairs in the filing

cabinet, just waiting for a calm, untroubling day.

A MARBLE RUN FOR ANOTHER END-OF-DAYS

I.

O bouquet of steak knives, I want you to uncut your own steel stems & grow again. This dry heat has taken all our fertile land

& we need you back in the ground, serrated & rooting, lush & alive. I wish I could undo what's been done to all of us.

I wish I could undo what's been done to our bodies, our homes, our backyards—filled exclusively with broken glass. Sure, a war is coming,

but the truth is, a war is always arriving, alive & dead at the same time—warring & warring, a truck trucking without brakes.

Who cut the brake lines if not a vengeful human? Every field is a potter's field. All we build are glass houses of ammunition in the sun.

Instead, someone should help me build glass houses to protect trans kids from rain, while their shirts hang on the laundry line out back.

Each spring I take off my shirt, step into a greenhouse I've built, bury my feet in the soil & scatter eggshells. Most things are about growth

& tending your own rotting roots. Most things are about staying alive while men want you dead. In this life, I recline between too drunk

& the landscape of my partner's favorite forest. I recline just to see that the sky is all blue platitudes. This is my life, glittering & full of pulse.

II.

This is my life & no one else's. Just a glittering Odysseus: take the booze out of my body & all that's left is a light show of sound, an occasional record scratch & pennies shaken in a ceramic bowl. Take the blood out of my body & what's left are scars shaped like cymbals about to crash.

My scars have always been about symbols, about a particular percussion. We've all made some music—felt ashamed of the raw noise. Older than I've ever been, I'm tired of pretending that I don't love dubstep & a nasty drop. I'm tired of pretending to be so serious, when my heart sounds like a synthesizer & everyone lays a head to my chest, sometimes.

When my partner lays their head to my chest, they remark on its steady rhythm. Yes, it snows in our bedroom, delicate & supernatural.

My partner's heart thumps like thunder thrown overboard, divine & unnatural. Astonishment & fear are dizzy sensations born of stomachs—seasick with mortality, dizzy with our skin in sun. I once told my partner that the ocean never learned to swim, so I built the water wings.

Though I've taken the ocean into my mouth, I still can't swim. O small & delicate avalanche in the bedroom, everything is about the heart.

III.

O steep & decisive avalanche, why don't you swallow our bodies & make them yours? My chest replicates the moon's rocky mist. My once-

breasts are flat & cold as the moon—cratered side of the pillow. Each morning, I blue from dreams of my life on the mountain: overdoses

& only ash. Each morning, my partner fevers, after a night captive in their Catholic school cafeteria. They touch me & their fever falls.

They touch me & I recall fire that took my body as kindling. My mother shoveled January into the tub & forced me in. I learned early

how to draw up an ice bath for whoever runs too hot. I learned young to mother both the hailing child & the colicky storm. Life, after all,

is about learning. Each hailstorm has an eye that can see more than we've ever seen. Isn't that incredible? When the end begins, we will run

& when we run, I'll mourn the houseplants, stuck in their pots. We've done most things terribly wrong: I pack my head wound with glitter

in the hope that I heal shining. I have most things so dreadfully wrong, except standing nearer to midnight & loving my partner. Always,

it's midnight & O bouquet of tulips dead on my counter, let me take that violence in my mouth, let me uncut your stems. Let's just grow again.

TO THE CHERRY BLOSSOMS ON 16TH AND WHARTON

I've written too many poems that assume
the trees I speak to cannot hear me, cannot

feel me. And of course they can. They are probably
hollering back, something about *kids these days*

and how I should certainly drink more water
and maybe give them some, too. When I picked

up my life and moved it to the city, it was for love.
Who hasn't put their life in a duffle bag and flown

toward something brighter than the sun. On 16th
and Wharton the cherry blossoms open in spring

and make a generally terrible world pink, and so
open to all my aspirations about marriage

and family. It is January now, and far too warm,
but what am I supposed to do besides take a walk

and hold my partner's hand? I am worried
the cherry blossoms will bloom too soon,

but then again, once, while in the desert,
I believed a cow's salt lick was a quartz

mortar and pestle. It is embarrassing
to understand so little about the world

while taking up all this space, but here I am,
whole and sturdy and committed to spring,

whenever it comes.

NOTES

The poem "One Hundred Demons" shares its title with Lynda Barry's 2005 graphic novel.

"For Mac Miller and 2009" takes references, and inspiration, from Mac Miller's songs and albums.

With long and sprawling lines, the marble run is a form I've designed that takes its shape from the antique toy of the same name. The second half of the first line is transformed in the first half of the second line, and so on. For three nine-line stanzas this pattern is sustained, until the twenty-seventh line, in which the second half of the poem's final line calls back to the first half of the poem's first line. For years, I used a Jacob's ladder toy to conceptualize the movement of a crown of sonnets. I wanted to apply the same logic to a new form.

"To the Cherry Blossoms on 16th and Wharton" is after Ross Gay's "To the Fig Tree on 9th and Christian."

ACKNOWLEDGMENTS

Thank you to the editors of the publications in which several of the poems in this book appeared, sometimes in different forms.

Academy of American Poets Poem-a-Day: "Daytona 500"

The Adroit Journal: "Elegy for the not yet dead Rainforest Cafe"

The American Poetry Review: "All in Red," "From Above," "A Marble Run for the Lights," "A Marble Run for This Finite Earth," and "One Hundred Demons"

Cherry Tree: "Y2K in NEPA"

DIAGRAM: "Haibun for My Mother and the Early 2000s"

Embodied: An Intersectional Feminist Comics Poetry Anthology: "To the Cherry Blossoms on 16th and Wharton"

Flypaper Lit: "A poem about only baseball"

Foglifter: "I wish I were more like my mother"

Frontier Poetry: "A Marble Run for Another End-of-Days"

Peach Mag: "Poem for the Start of a New Decade"

Ploughshares and Winning Writers: "Ghazals connected as though cargo freights"

Puerto del Sol: "On imagining Ariana Grande, before the fame, working every summer at Rita's Italian Ice"

Southeast Review: "The only atlas we need is one drafted by children," "A poem about Batman," and "Silent Light"

TriQuarterly: "Ghazal Written for the Lids in Downtown Brooklyn Where I Chose My Name"

The West Review: "Another Poem about Cornfields"

THANKS

I'd like to give immense thanks to the Copper Canyon team for their support and for their continued belief in my work, with special thanks given to Ashley E. Wynter. Working with you has been such a gift—a gift that's made this process so fun and has made the work so much stronger.

Endless gratitude to the Pew Foundation, the National Endowment for the Arts, the Leeway Foundation, and the Carolyn Moore Writing Residency for the support that made this book of poems possible.

To my beautiful friends: thank you for your enduring love and light. I am so very lucky to be on this big, spinning rock with all of you. And to all the friends no longer here: I miss you every day. This book is for you.

To my matriarchs: Kristine Conners, Valerie Griffith, and Rachel Lapidus, thank you for showing me the way—again and again.

And to Jack Papanier, there are no words that can describe the good fortune of sharing a life with you. I'm spellbound every day. Thank you for sharing your magic with me.

ABOUT THE AUTHOR

 Kayleb Rae Candrilli is the recipient of a Whiting Award, a Pew fellowship, and a fellowship from the National Endowment for the Arts. They are the author of *Water I Won't Touch, All the Gay Saints,* and *What Runs Over.* Candrilli lives in Philadelphia with their partner. Photo by Ryan Collerd, courtesy of The Pew Center for Arts & Heritage.

Poetry is vital to language and living. Since 1972, Copper Canyon Press has published extraordinary poetry from around the world to engage the imaginations and intellects of readers, writers, booksellers, librarians, teachers, students, and donors.

WE ARE GRATEFUL FOR THE MAJOR SUPPORT PROVIDED BY:

academy of
american poets

OFFICE OF ARTS & CULTURE
SEATTLE

ARTSFUND

THE PAUL G. ALLEN
FAMILY FOUNDATION

Hawthornden
Foundation

POETRY
FOUNDATION

INGRAM
CONTENT GROUP

the point
envision · enact · evolve

McSWEENEY'S

WASHINGTON STATE
ARTS COMMISSION

  National
Endowment
for the Arts
arts.gov
ART WORKS.

The Witter Bynner Foundation
for Poetry

TO LEARN MORE ABOUT UNDERWRITING
COPPER CANYON PRESS TITLES,
PLEASE CALL 360-385-4925 EXT. 105

WE ARE GRATEFUL FOR THE MAJOR SUPPORT PROVIDED BY:

Anonymous

Jill Baker and Jeffrey Bishop

Anne and Geoffrey Barker

Donna Bellew

Will Blythe

John Branch

Diana Broze

John R. Cahill

Sarah J. Cavanaugh

Keith Cowan and Linda Walsh

Peter Currie

The Evans Family

Mimi Gardner Gates

Gull Industries Inc.
    on behalf of William True

Carolyn and Robert Hedin

David and Jane Hibbard

Bruce S. Kahn

Phil Kovacevich and Eric Wechsler

Maureen Lee and Mark Busto

Ellie Mathews and Carl Youngmann
    as The North Press

Larry Mawby and Lois Bahle

Petunia Charitable Fund and
    adviser Elizabeth Hebert

Suzanne Rapp and Mark Hamilton

Adam and Lynn Rauch

Emily and Dan Raymond

Joseph C. Roberts

Cynthia Sears

Kim and Jeff Seely

Tree Swenson

Julia Sze

Barbara and Charles Wright

In honor of C.D. Wright
    from Forrest Gander

Caleb Young as C. Young Creative

The dedicated interns and faithful
    volunteers of Copper Canyon Press

The pressmark for Copper Canyon Press
suggests entrance, connection, and interaction
while holding at its center
an attentive, dynamic space for poetry.

This book is set in Bourton Hand and Than.
Book design and composition by
Becca Fox Design and Claretta Holsey.
Printed on archival-quality paper.